JILL OLIVER

Flipping Houses For A Profit Or Losing Your Shirt In The Process

Learn the Pitfalls of Flipping Houses

This book was professionally typeset on Reedsy.
Find out more at reedsy.com

Contents

Introduction

hy did I write this book? I want to let the average person know that flipping houses is a risky business. I am a real estate professional and thought I knew enough to make wise decisions about the market, repairs, contractors etc and to my surprise I was just another person that had gotten caught up in the hype of flipping houses. I had even attended a 2-3 day seminar and paid a hefty fee for all the calculators , spreadsheets and connections and beautiful illustrations that comprised the course. I thought the process would be seamless. Low and behold I had many sleepless nights trying to keep myself from drowning in the sea of flipping houses.

Now don't get me wrong or think of me as a hater. I don't doubt that many investors made nice profits flipping houses but I haven't met anyone. All the people I encountered trying to flip a house either lost money or broke even and decided to invest in something else besides flipping houses.

Flipping History

W**hat is house flipping anyway and where did this concept come from**:

Flipping used to be a dirty word when it referred to houses. Back in the 80's and 90's there were lazed laws surrounding house flipping that weren't being enforced so investors took advantage of low income, uneducated people. They used unscrupulous tactics to buy and sell properties which eventually resulted in foreclosures and costing the government lots of money.

So here is one scenario for you: An investor would purchase a home from someone in trouble with their mortgage or someone who didn't want to do any work to the house and agreed to sell it cheap or for pennies on the dollar. The investor would offer quick closings and help to take the house off the seller's hands quickly. This was very desirable to a seller that had a mess of a house to sell or in the midst of a foreclosure.

Once the investor acquired the property, they would look for a buyer to purchase the property, preferably a first time home buyer with bad credit and little to no knowledge of the home buying process. The investor would work hard to gain the trust of the prospective home buyer with their questionable sales tactics and promise to arrange the financing and closing for them, even going as far as lending the prospect money to close the deal. This, by the way, was against the law. The buyers didn't know until it was too late that the investor purchased the property for pennies on the dollar and did the minimal amount of cosmetic work make the property seem to be in good condition. They then found themselves with a mortgage loan that was inflated and a house that was not worth the money. Long story short, the new homeowners were unable to keep the homes up due to repairs and over higher than usual monthly payments. Many home owners had no choice but to forfeit on their loans. The foreclosures left people homeless, neighborhoods blighted and a myriad of community issues

Some of the protections were put in place by the Federal Housing Administration to protect low income buyers from Flipping schemes:

The Federal Housing Administration will not back up a loan to the lending institution if the property was resold in less than 90 days of purchase. In addition if the price was more than 100 percent of the purchase price the house would need to be appraised more than once and the underwriters were requiring receipts for major renovations done on the property.

Professionals such as real estate professionals, loan officers and appraisers found themselves serving jail sentences and having their licenses revoked.

After the laws around flipping houses were strengthened and defined, flipping slowed down and took on a new reputation. Thanks to reality TV.

Let's fast forward to around 2005. A&E debuted what's believed to be the first show "Flip this House" and soon after HGTV followed with "Flip or Flop" and "Flipping Virgins". From there we have been inundated with construction shows and a lot of house flipping and designing shows. There were so many flipping shows that everyone you talked to wanted to try their hand at it.

Today the flipping shows are still going strong with at least 11 on Netflix alone. These shows are so powerful and seem to be so realistic and relatable that it gets one's creative juices flowing and people start telling themselves that if these people can flip houses so can they. Here are some of the shows streaming today:

Flip or Flop
Design Today
Tidying up with Marie Kondo
Fixer Upper
House Hunters International
Design on a Dime
House Hunters
Beach Front Bargain Hunt
Genevieve's Renovation

There are plenty of books and courses that are available to tell you how great it is to flip properties.

So You Think Flipping Is For You

Don't Believe the hype:

Once you get hooked on the shows and convince yourself, your spouse, some friends and maybe some family members and decide that you have what it takes to Flip some houses , it's on. Even if you're told not to do it, you'll probably try it anyway. So let's get started. The first question to ask yourself is how will I finance my project? Will I pay cash, take out a mortgage on your home, borrow from a 401 K or borrow from a Hard Money Lender.It might sound far-fetched but there are a lot of people out.

It might sound far-fetched but there are a lot of people out here that have access to lots of money and they were spending it on these flips.

So let's look at some of the ways people financed their flips:

Cash is king so lets start there. If you had a 100k to 200k sitting in the bank or could get a couple of people together with that kind of money you could finance your flip with the cash and save on all the lenders fees and the risk of not getting the project completed on time. On the flip side I have seen people over improve the property or drag the process out too long because they did not have to answer to anyone in regards to paying back the money at a designated time and rate. It also is risky because you may be spending your life savings and if things don't go as planned you just lost money that you may not have the means to get back.

Another option I heard being tossed around a lot was borrowing money from your 401K. It seems as if you can buy a house, pay for improvements and even sell the house or flip the house. This is something you should talk to a financial planner or a CPA about because there are pros and cons to using your 401k to purchase properties to flip. Since everyone has a unique situation you would not want to follow someone's lead on this

In addition to using cash or 401K, investors unloaded the equity from their homes to get into the flipping market. This can be a way to borrow money at a reasonable rate since it is backed by your home or in some cases a rental property. You need to have good credit and a sizable amount of equity in your home. This is referred to as a HELOC or Home Equity Line of Credit. A HELOC loan might give 80% loan to value and one of the beauties of this loan is that you only pay interest when you use it and carry a balance and once you pay it back you can use the money again and again without applying each time you need it.

The most used loan to finance flips by far was the Hard Money Loan. This loan had little to no regulations and the terms were mostly ridiculous and sucked a large portion of the profit out of the deal. A Hard Money Loan had the worst terms you could imagine and yet extremely popular. The lenders only lent you their money if you agreed to terms that could easily have them take your house and all that you invested in it if you were not able to pay the money back in sometimes 6–12 months. If you went past the deadline they may agree to give you an extension and charge you thousands of dollars extra. This was risky business at its worst and so many people chose this option rather than to pass up the chance of flipping a property, me included.

Lets Get Started

Starting the Process:

So the next thing an investor should ask themselves is what kind of properties do you want to flip. Is it single family detached homes? Is it row houses or town homes? What price range are you willing to consider and what areas do you want to flip houses in. So many times I've spoken to investors who had no idea the answers to any of these questions. They just wanted to make money. I would tell them investing in real estate is a business and you need to figure out what that looks like to you. Just saying you want to make money off of properties is not enough. Truth be told we all want to make money and if the deal is that good everyone would be trying to purchase it, including me. This is where a lot of Flippers go wrong. They listen to other investors bragging about their deals and what they are doing to get you all excited so they can unload some of their bad investments on you. This happens a lot with junk properties in terrible neighborhoods.I've had plenty of investors tell me they heard that they can buy a house in Baltimore for 5K (that's where I was living at the time) and I would tell them yes you can but what are you going to do with it? You'll need more money than it's worth to rehab it and then it's in the middle of a war zone so who's buying it from you since that's the only way to make money? My advice is to take some time and decide what you would want to invest in and find a few neighborhoods that your money would land you a good property with enough left to renovate and complete a desirable property to sell.

Once you have a good idea of what you want to invest in, it's time to decide how you'll find your first property to flip. Will it be with the help of a Real Estate agent or at an auction or maybe from a wholesaler or by searching the public records and sending letters or cold calling. As you can see there are many ways to find houses to flip, unfortunately the more investors in the marketplace the more the prices are driven upwards. This makes it difficult to purchase a property for the right price.

The right price will be a price that will allow you to purchase the property and rehab it with a design and finishes that will bring you top dollar in the marketplace and a profit in line with what you bargained for.

Although using a Real Estate agent is sometimes undesirable to an investor since they have fees that will cut into your bottom line, they have connections that can often land you a deal that no one else is privy to. For instance, a real estate agent may know of someone selling their property for a deep discount because they don't choose to make any repairs and by the way, they inherited the house. When you seek out a Real Estate agent, take time to research who is buying investments in the areas you are interested in and you may be surprised to find that one or two companies or real estate agents are selling all of them. You may want to start talking to them. These Agents you identified evidently know what is going on in the area which is why they have what is called, Market Share. You would have to determine if they have time to work with another investor. They may be able to show you other areas that you didn't realize were hot for flipping houses. At the same time you can be frequenting the auction sites for possible deals. You can simultaneously look for houses on the market, off the market, at auctions etc. Just do your homework. Auctions for one are very risky if you don't have cash on hand. If you make a deposit at an auction you are expected to pay the balance in a specified time and if you cannot pay you lose the non refundable deposit and no there are no contingencies. There are no appraisals or home inspections for the most part.

Some investors rather purchase from a wholesaler who peddles mostly junk properties. Most of these properties are flipped from one person to another while adding a substantial fee to the price and never taking ownership. Once in a while an investor can find a wholesale property that they can flip for a profit. I know you've seen the signs littering the side of the road "WE BUY HOUSES", it is illegal in most jurisdictions to place these signs on public property but investors love these signs because they bring calls and prospective sellers to their phones. With the help of telemarketers, investors can pay people minimum wages with bonus incentives to find properties off market. These properties can have deep discounts. The bottom line is whatever you do to find your properties make sure you buy the property for the right price or you're going to lose your shirt. If the cost of the property and the cost of the rehab is more than 70% of the after repair value, walk away quickly, You will lose money.

In the midst of finding where you want to invest, how you will get the money, who will be assisting you and so on, you will also need to be doing your due diligence at all times. Finding a mentor can be a great idea. Sometimes people want to see others succeed and have knowledge that they are willing to share. Keep in mind that everyone has a different idea of investing so take what you can from them but stick to your guns on the things you know that can cause you to lose your shirt.

Limiting The Risk

Educate Yourself:

Open your mind and learn all that you can before plunging into the Flipping arena. Once you get started there is no turning back at least until your project is finished and that can be 6 months to a year depending on the project. There are hundreds of books and learning material for you to study. I still see seminars being advertised. Don't forget there are investor groups you can join but beware of folks trying to get you to buy properties from them that they know will be duds. You could find and link up with other investors that will let you view their properties that are in the process of being renovated. Investors love to brag about their work. At the end of the day , If you're anything like me, once you study a bit and think you got it, you're going to push the button and get started and that is exactly what I did.

Pitfalls

The problems with Flipping houses

Contractors

One of the most important things to this whole venture is finding contractors. Good , solid contractors are so hard to find. Oh, there are a lot of them out there but they can wreck your project really quickly. One horror story was about a lady I met when I went to her open house and the renovation she did to her house was very impressive. She took the time to tell me she had a contractor that ran off with 30K dollars of her money. He convinced her that it was customary to put down a certain amount before the repairs were started and she gave him a sizable amount of money and he never came back.

Some investors prefer small contracting companies and some with larger more established companies. In my experience , If you hire a small company and don't have their undivided attention, they will try and do several jobs while doing yours without enough manpower to get all the jobs done in the agreed time frame. On the flip side, if you use a large company, in my experience, they can be too costly. Believe it or not, you can still have major issues with a large contracting company as well. You can always sue a company if they don't perform as agreed however time is of the essence so Investors are focused on getting the job done to cash out and go to the next project. Investors don't necessarily have time for the court stuff. You can try and bypass this kind of headache by getting recent referrals and taking field trips to observe contractor's work which would be the best advice I can give. It's still a gamble even after all of that.

After you do your due diligence vetting contractors they still can be very scary to work with. For some reason many of them don't possess a good work ethic. It's the strangest thing. The work they perform may be superb but you may have to make sure they show up and do the work like a babysitter. Then you have some that just quit on you in the middle of the project and never come back, or answer their phones. I've had a contractor damage the roof putting up a vent for the plumbing and had water leaking from the roof after the drywall, ceilings and recessed lights were installed. Although it was the plumber's fault he did not want to fix it.I ran into this a lot where the contractors really did not want to pull permits with the municipalities so they would offer to do the work without pulling permits, for a reduced price. That was a huge no no for me since I am not a contractor and had no idea how the work should have been done. I wanted to feel confident that the work was done correctly which meant paying for permits and having a licensed inspection check the house to make sure the repairs were done properly. Also keep in mind that many of the people saying they are contractors do not possess a license, they work under someone else's license which can cost you a premium since the real contractor has to be paid as well.

Buying the house too high

Enough about the contractors there are other issues that can make your flip a flop. The other one that is not as obvious is paying too much for the house in the first place. Just imagine you decided to flip a house, you know where and how you're going to get the financing and now you just have to find that house. You are almost willing to take anything that sounds halfway good to get started. After all you have been binge watching all the Flipping shows on TV and now frequenting the investment groups.

This is when your emotions get the best of you. It's easy to compromise on the numbers and forget to stick to your guns. This is when your emotions have you seriously considering a house that is more like 75% of the ARV (After repair value) minus the cost of repairs. This is more than what you should pay for a property you intend to flip and now the entire project is in jeopardy. If any problems arise and they will, it will eat into the profits that have already been reduced since you purchased the property for too much. You will be constantly trying to find ways to cut expenses and that usually does not work out in your favor.

Underestimating the cost of repairs

If you're really serious about making money in this business it is wise to invest in a software program that will do a cost estimate for your project. Remember, an estimator is only good as the information it is fed. Some of the programs on the market are Investor's Edge, Flipper Force and Property Fixer to name a few. This will save you a lot of time and if all goes well with the project, like not too many hiccups, your project should be close to the estimate. Sorry to say this is often not the case. Even with a 10% cushion that is added to the cost of the repairs, the repairs usually run over. Too often it's for a repair or replacement that is non negotiable. For example, I have a friend who was flipping houses and had one house where robbers broke in and stole all the stainless steel appliances from the house. They had to be replaced. No appliances would have had a negative effect on the marketing and sale of the house. I've witnessed a situation where the contractors did not call out the City inspector prior to starting the deck in the back of the house and had to tear it down and start over again. More lumber had to be purchased and more labor costs were incurred. Who would've thought that in one row house contractors were taking down the tiles in the bathroom, causing the tiles in the next door neighbor's house to fall off the wall and that had to be paid for.

As you can see there are some many things that can happen to start running up the bill on your flip. Many of the adages you never could have estimated in the calculations. This is what makes flipping houses a dangerous game.

Changing Market Conditions

I bet you never considered that this could hurt your bottom line but it most certainly can. How about you purchase a house to Flip in November and you are timing it just right to start the project in December but the weather is too bad for part of December, January and February and you lose a total of 30 days of working on the house. Once you get back to moving and shaking on the project, you notice that the interest rates are inching upwards and the house prices are falling some. Now instead of having a house to market in March or April it's been pushed back to July. Historically, the best market is in the spring and the fall of the year. Because of the delays experienced by the investor the project is pushed back. Now the Flipper can expect for there to be less buyers in the marketplace and the Sellers' market that existed when the house was purchased has lost its steam and will no longer be as strong. Scenarios like this can really sink your ship. This is a snowball effect that started with the bad weather and caused the sale of the house to be pushed back enough to miss the best market. Unbeknownst to many people the real estate market can change really fast. It can fluctuate through changing markets like it will go from a buyers to sellers market in a few months and it can be for various reasons like rising interest rates, inflation or supply and demand. A flip that is not on schedule will definitely have a different outcome than projected. It's very unlikely going to be a favorable outcome since time is money.

Hard Money Loan

While on the subject of money let's talk about these Hard Money Loans in more detail. So they are like borrowing from a loan shark . Loan Sharks were known to lend money and hunt you down for repayment, sometimes breaking your bones in the process. I wouldn't say a Hard Money Lender is as scary as that however, the terms are unconventional to say the least. What is appealing about them is that if you were recommended, they came with a solid plan and a project that seemed like it would make money and they would finance your deal. It is very different from a loan on a property you plan to live in. I did not mention that the loan was at a high interest rate, required an upfront investment, high monthly payments and a full repayment date in as little as 6-12 months. If you failed to repay the loan in full by the due date the hard money lender would consider extending the terms of your loan and charging you a hefty fee to do so. Like a few thousand dollars. When borrowing money this way you were taking on a partner without knowing it. If you just couldn't pay off the loan the hard money lenders would take the house, finish it up and sell it. All your hard work, time and money went down the drain. There were other loans that were not as vicious to the investors but it took more time and energy to secure them.The Hard Money Lenders were able to close loans in a few days. While trying to choose and secure a loan the flipping market was on fire and waiting for no one. The Hard Money Loan was looking good with the quickest funding time with the largest risk of all.

Real Estate Professionals

While many investors heavily rely on real estate agents to find them properties to flip, they try their hardest to sell the finished products themselves to save money and improve their bottom line. As a real estate professional, I would say this is where you can recoup some of the money that went down the drain in the process of rehabbing the property. I know this sounds backwards because a real estate brokerage is going to charge you money to sell your house but they can use their expertise to get the best possible offer from the best prospective buyer and have it sold quickly. The real estate professional really knows the market and can do creative things to market the property for optimal results.. Not all agents are created equal so this is the time to do your due diligence and find someone that loves the work you did and wants to not only sell your property but sees the benefit in building a relationship with you. This could lead to a broker shaving down some of their commission in hopes of becoming your exclusive agent. As good as a real estate agent can be for your project's success, you can hire a deadbeat that can drag your project out even longer by not being mentally and physically available or not advertising the property or creating a plan for maximum exposure that would lead to a quick sale. I would recommend refraining from using family members that have licenses they never use until you need your flip sold. If you want the assistance of a real estate professional, find one who knows the market and the area and is willing to roll up their sleeves and partner with you to get the listing sold at the highest possible price.

Design flop

I would be remiss if I did not mention a design flop as one of the many pitfalls of flipping houses. Not only did the house flipping shows give the average viewer courage to flip houses, they also gave many people the idea that they were designers and could design a house.that would be appealing to a home buyer. Since I was selling real estate at the time the big flipping craze was in full swing, I viewed a lot of rehabbed homes and some were spectacular where others were poorly designed. The ones that were poorly designed or rehabbed with questionable taste, got passed over by the masses of the house hunters. One house in particular, I remember, the stairs from the first floor to the second floor were so steep I was scared to climb the stairs. Not only were they steep, they were extremely narrow. Surprisingly the craftsmanship put into rehabbing the house was great with very appealing finishes. The way the house was designed caused the house to sit empty for some time.. I believe it stayed on the market for years until the right person came along and purchased it. Wow, that was a bummer for some investors. I actually had the listing on the house for a while and I hosted a tour where at least a hundred potential home buyers viewed the home and no one made an offer.

I've also witnessed where the investors removed the bathtub from the main bathroom and only had showers in the house. This is not a total flop but it can turn off prospective buyers. Most home buyers want the option to bathe at some point and if they're thinking about resale value, no tub can be a turn off. In addition to the design of the house, I saw many houses that had poor workmanship. Renovations looked like they were completed by an amateur. The worst thing to see when walking into a rehab is a horrible drywall and paint job. Not to mention all around poor workmanship. You could tell that they did a patch job and did not tear down and rebuild. That can work in some instances where the house just needs cosmetics and freshened up. To get your flip to shine in the end you need the right design, finishes and a house stage with a track record. More money, more money $$$

Conclusion

I'm sure you picked up on the fact that I am a real estate professional. I sold real estate for many years and my husband and I are investors. We have a few properties that we want to pass to our children. We flipped 3 houses and promised not to ever do it again. I lost plenty of sleepless nights and miserable days worrying about finishing those 3 properties and getting them sold. I mean it is really scary because much of your control is out of your hands. You're relying on the contractors, inspectors, lenders etc. When you're used to running your own show this is scary. I did learn a great deal and I am so grateful that I was able to sell all 3 of the houses to homeowners, but I cannot say I was one of the fortunate ones who made a profit. It was a bittersweet time for me because I was so grateful to be able to see the projects through to the end but I lost my shirt in the process. Luckily I had family to bale me out with no long term effects.

My husband and I do much better with buying and holding until the market is right. When everyone is running one way we normally walk the other way. We have had success with small multi unit properties over the years and now we use the rents to supplement our income.

This book is just a way to get you thinking that there's more to Flipping houses than what is being portrayed on television. If you still need to fulfill your fantasy, do your best to educate yourself and make decisions that mitigate the risk and don't forget to watch out for the landmines. You may just come out a winner!